I0821645

ANIMAL ALBUMS

THE SHARK FAMILY

BY GOLRIZ GOLKAR

eureka!

EUREKA!, AN IMPRINT OF BELLWETHER MEDIA BY FLUTTERBEE

Eureka! books turn real stories into unforgettable experiences. Clear, direct language and sharp, captivating imagery make it easy to follow your curiosity, one fascinating fact at a time. Your Eureka! moment awaits!

For information regarding permission, write to Bellwether Media, Inc., Attention: Permissions Department, 3500 American Blvd W, Suite 150, Bloomington, MN 55431.

Library of Congress Cataloging-in-Publication Data is available at www.loc.gov or upon request from the publisher.

ISBN: 9798893048575 (hardcover)
ISBN: 9798893049572 (ebook)

Editor: Rebecca Sabelko   Designer: Josh Brink   Series Designer: Jeff Kollock

Printed in the United States of America, North Mankato, MN.

TABLE OF
CONTENTS

WHAT ARE SHARKS?

Sharks are a subclass of fish called *Elasmobranchii*. There are more than 500 shark species.

Like other fish, most sharks are cold-blooded vertebrates. All sharks have fins. They breathe through gills. Most sharks have five gills on each side of their head, but some have six or seven. Unlike other fish, sharks have skeletons made from cartilage rather than bone.

Most sharks live in salt water, including all five oceans on Earth. Others live well in less salty coastal waters. A few species can survive in freshwater rivers and lakes.

BULL SHARK in a freshwater river

KINGDOM
ANIMALIA

PHYLUM
CHORDATA

CLASS
CHONDRICHTHYES

SUBCLASS
ELASMOBRANCHII

ORDERS
CARCHARHINIFORMES, HETERODONTIFORMES, HEXANCHIFORMES, LAMNIFORMES, ORECTOLOBIFORMES, PRISTIOPHORIFORMES, SQUALIFORMES, SQUATINIFORMES

TAXONOMY CHART

TIGER SHARK ▲

▲ WHITE SHARK

THE HISTORY OF
SHARKS

The earliest remains of sharklike animals date to about 450 million years ago. These animals had denticles but no teeth. Around 359 million years ago, many shark species survived a mass extinction. More types started to evolve. Modern sharks first appeared around 200 million years ago. The largest sharks to ever live evolved around 20 million years ago. Megalodons reached up to 80 feet (24 meters) long!

MEGALODON TOOTH

FANCY FEATURES

Some sharks have unique adaptations that help them survive. Spiracles are little holes behind their eyes that draw water toward their gills. Barbels are whisker-like organs that help some find food.

BARBELS

Sharks' adaptations have made them successful. The evolution to eat many different foods is one of their biggest successes. Their torpedo shape, rows of teeth, special senses, and many other adaptations also make them fit for survival.

EVOLUTIONARY EXCELLENCE

SNOUT
has electrical sensors that help sharks detect prey

DORSAL FIN
helps sharks keep their balance

PECTORAL FINS
help sharks lift, turn, and brake

TAIL FIN
helps sharks move fast in water

LATERAL LINE
helps sharks sense movement in water and find prey

LIFE CYCLE

Most shark species give birth to live babies called pups. Some sharks have one or two pups in a litter. Others, such as blue sharks, may have more than 100. Sharks usually have babies once every two to three years.

▲ BLUE SHARK

▲ PREGNANT BULL SHARK

NEWBORN SPINY DOGFISH SHARK ▼

Some species are born from eggs. Females lay eggs encased in leathery pouches in safe places such as seaweed or coral reefs. In other species, pups grow in eggs inside their mothers' bodies. When the eggs hatch, the pups continue to grow inside their mothers' bodies until they are born. Pups are on their own after they are born.

▲ SHARK EGG

AVERAGE LITTER SIZE

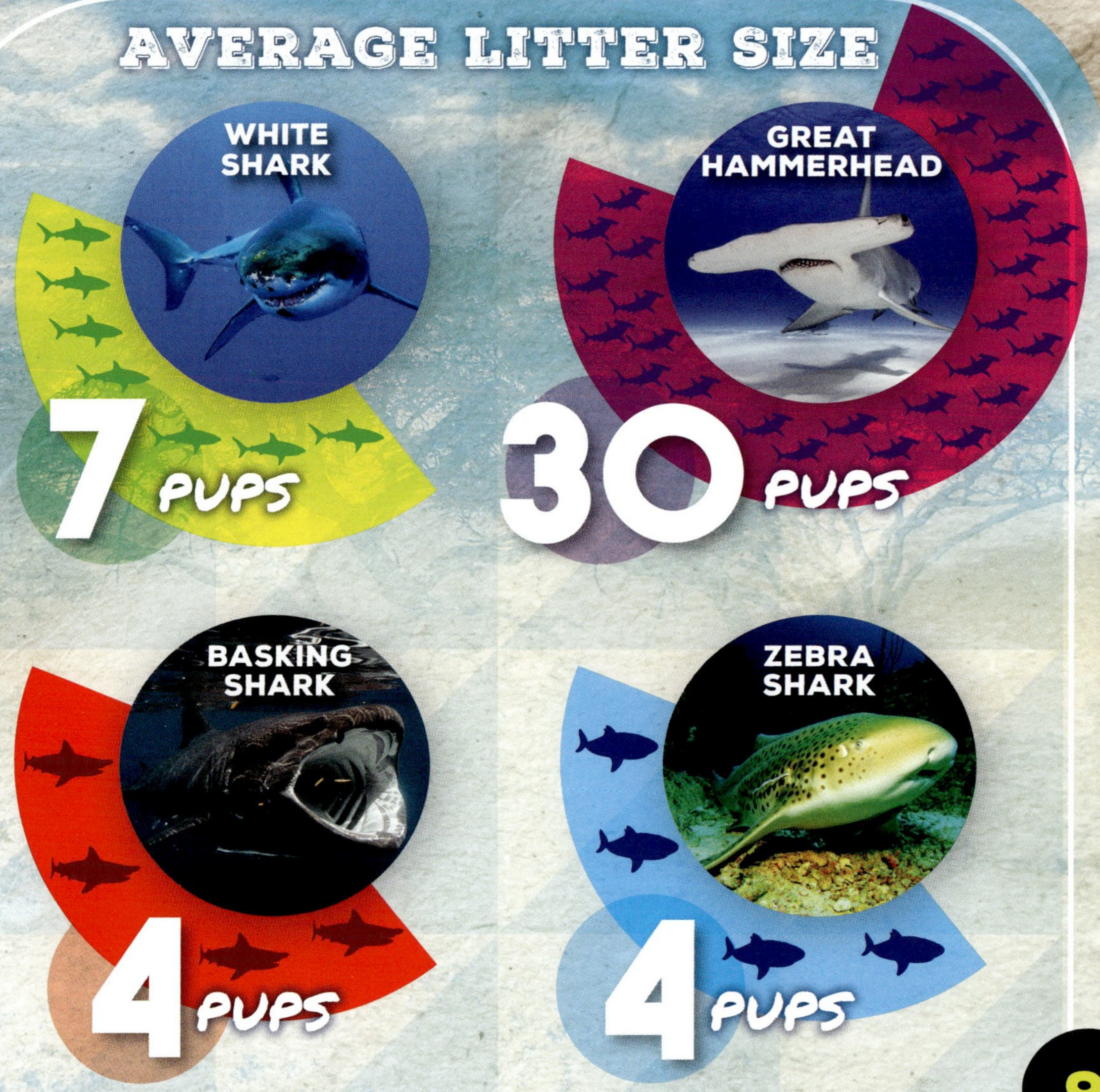

WHITE SHARK
7 PUPS

GREAT HAMMERHEAD
30 PUPS

BASKING SHARK
4 PUPS

ZEBRA SHARK
4 PUPS

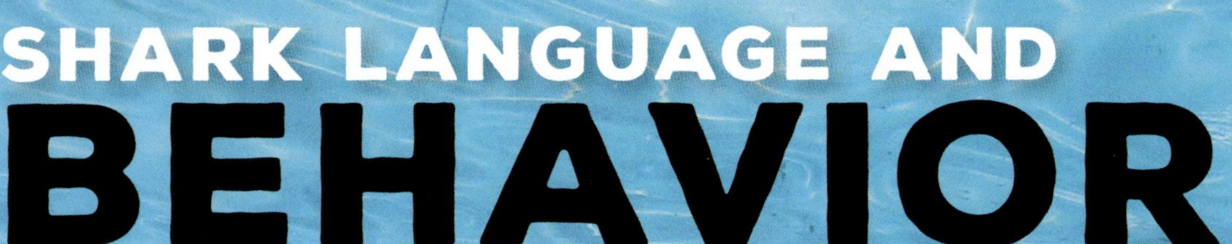

SHARK LANGUAGE AND BEHAVIOR

BEHAVIORS AND COMMUNICATION

Sharks use body language to communicate. Some arch their backs or open their mouths at the water's surface to warn enemies to stay away. They may slap their tails on the water's surface to show their strength. This is common when they compete for food.

MALE NURSE SHARK
biting a female's fin

Female sharks release chemicals when they are ready to mate. Male sharks are then drawn to the scent of the chemicals. Males may leap out of the water to attract females. Sometimes, they bite females' fins during mating.

TIGER SHARK

BLACKTIP REEF SHARK

MIGRATION

Sharks usually migrate to follow prey. They may swim to warmer waters as temperatures change. Some migrate to find a mate.

WHALE SHARK

SHARK FAMILY TREE

GROUND SHARKS

OVER 250 SPECIES

HAMMERHEAD SHARKS ▲

▲TIGER SHARKS

Tiger sharks sometimes feed on other sharks and dead fish.

BULL SHARKS ▲

Bull sharks can camouflage well in sunlight and shadows.

CARPET SHARKS

AROUND 40 SPECIES

WHALE SHARKS ▲

Whale sharks are gentle and harmless to humans.

▲ZEBRA SHARKS

▲NURSE SHARKS

BULLHEAD SHARKS

9 SPECIES

HORN SHARKS ▶

ELASMOBRANCHII

MACKEREL SHARKS
AROUND 15 SPECIES

▲ BASKING SHARKS

▲ WHITE SHARKS

FRILLED AND COW SHARKS
6 SPECIES

Frilled and cow sharks are some of the oldest kinds of sharks alive today.

SAWSHARKS
8 SPECIES

▲ BAHAMAS SAWSHARKS

DOGFISH SHARK
AT LEAST 130 SPECIES

▲ COOKIECUTTER SHARKS

Some species of dogfish sharks are venomous. They have two sharp spines by each dorsal fin that release venom.

ANGEL SHARKS
AT LEAST 24 SPECIES

SHARK BIOGRAPHIES

HAMMERHEAD SHARKS

There are 10 species of hammerhead sharks. Their wide heads make them specialized hunters.

SCALLOPED HAMMERHEAD

WHERE DO THEY LIVE?

Hammerheads live in warm, shallow waters in temperate or tropical areas. They are often found near reefs, coasts, and lagoons.

GREAT HAMMERHEAD
Range in the Wild

● = Range

PINNED!

Great hammerheads pin down stingrays with their wide heads.

SIZE COMPARISON

20FT (6.1 m)	13FT (4 m)	10FT (3 m)
great hammerhead	bull shark 	Atlantic nurse shark 

APPEARANCE

These sharks have olive green to gray-brown backs and white bellies. They have flat hammer-shaped heads with wide-set eyes. The first dorsal fin is curved with a pointed tip. Some species have very tall dorsal fins.

DIET

These sharks eat stingrays, shrimp, and crabs. The undersides of their wide heads can sense prey's electric signals.

GREAT HAMMERHEAD

VULNERABLE SPECIES

▼ VULNERABLE TO CRITICALLY ENDANGERED ▼

THREATS

commercial fishing

pollution

climate change

habitat loss

CONSERVATION EFFORTS ▼

population and habitat monitoring

education about sharks

general ocean conservation

BONNETHEAD SHARK

TIGER SHARKS

Tiger sharks get their name from their stripes that fade as they grow older.

APPEARANCE

Tiger sharks have wide, short snouts and large tail fins. Their backs are gray, blue green, black, or brown. They have light bellies.

SIZE COMPARISON

18FT (5.5 m)

tiger shark

13FT (4 m)

bull shark

4FT (1.2 m)

horn shark

DIET

Tiger sharks are ambush hunters that use their stripes as camouflage. Their serrated teeth and powerful jaws help them finish their prey. They mostly eat dolphins, rays, and smaller fish. They also scavenge for food.

WHERE DO THEY LIVE?

Tiger sharks are found in all tropical waters except the Mediterranean Sea. They prefer shallow waters near coral reefs and seagrasses. They migrate with the seasons.

FAMOUS TIGER SHARK

KAMAKAI

- **Where does she live?**
  South Pacific Ocean

- **Famous for:**
  Kamakai is believed to be the world's largest tiger shark. Most tiger sharks grow to about 12 feet (3.7 meters) long. But Kamakai is around 18 feet (5.5 meters) long. Her large size makes it hard for her to move her fins, making her a slow swimmer.

BIG SHARK

Tiger sharks are one of the largest shark species. They can weigh more than 2,000 pounds (907 kilograms).

BULL SHARKS

Bull sharks are large, aggressive, and dangerous.

APPEARANCE

Bull sharks have short snouts and round, muscular bodies. Large, wide pectoral fins stick out from their gray-brown bodies. Their bellies are white.

RAGING BULL

Bull sharks often headbutt their prey before attacking it like a bull. This rough habit gives these sharks their name.

SIZE COMPARISON

40FT (12 m)

basking shark

13FT (4 m)

bull shark

2.8FT (0.9 m)

Bahamas sawshark

WHERE DO THEY LIVE?

Bull sharks are some of the only sharks that live in both salt water and fresh water. Some migrate thousands of miles up rivers. Others live in estuaries and tropical oceans.

DIET

Bull sharks are fast and powerful swimmers. They burst forward to catch prey with their strong jaws and knifelike teeth. They mostly feed on fish and small sharks.

FAMOUS BULL SHARKS

The Carbrook Sharks

Location:
Carbrook, Queensland, Australia

Famous for:
After major floods in 1996, at least six bull sharks swam into a lake on Carbrook Golf Club's course. Floodwaters dried up, and the path back to the ocean stayed closed for 17 years. The sharks were trapped in the lake. Sightings of the sharks ended after a 2013 flood.

HORN SHARKS

Horn sharks get their name from the sharp, venomous horns on their dorsal fins.

APPEARANCE

Horn sharks are small. Their horns warn predators to stay away. These sharks are gray or brown with dark spots and pale undersides. Pectoral fins help them crawl along the seafloor.

HORN

BIG BITE

Horn sharks have the strongest bite force of any shark relative to their size.

SIZE COMPARISON

9.8FT (3 m)	4FT (1.2 m)	2.8FT (0.9 m)
broadnose sevengill shark	horn shark	Bahamas sawshark

WHERE DO THEY LIVE?

Horn sharks live in the eastern Pacific Ocean. They often remain hidden in kelp beds, rocky crevices, and reefs.

HORN SHARK RELATIVE

GALÁPAGOS BULLHEAD SHARK

- **Range:** Peru and the Galápagos Islands
- **Known for:** These sharks are poor swimmers, so they move very little. They use their large pectoral fins to crawl slowly along seabeds. They are the only egg-laying sharks in the Galápagos. Both horn sharks and Galápagos bullhead sharks lay spiral-shaped egg cases.

HORN SHARK EGG CASE

DIET

Horn sharks hunt at night. They mostly eat mollusks and crustaceans. Tubelike jaws use suction to capture prey. Wide back teeth powerfully crush shells.

BROADNOSE SEVENGILL SHARKS

Broadnose sevengill sharks have changed very little since they first appeared around 195 million years ago.

WHERE DO THEY LIVE?

Broadnose sevengill sharks live in shallow, temperate coastal waters in parts of the Atlantic, Pacific, and Indian Oceans. They sometimes migrate to mate and follow prey.

BROADNOSE SEVENGILL SHARK
Range in the Wild

= Range

SIZE COMPARISON

9.8FT (3 m)

broadnose sevengill shark

59FT (18 m)

whale shark

13FT (4 m)

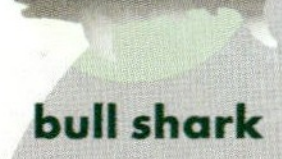

bull shark

APPEARANCE

Broadnose sevengill sharks have broad heads and snouts. While most sharks have five gills, these sharks have seven. Black-and-white spots cover their grayish-brown bodies.

DIET

These sharks sometimes hunt in small groups. They attack seals and sharks. They hunt smaller prey, such as bony fish, alone. They stalk small prey before ambushing them.

VULNERABLE SPECIES

▼ VULNERABLE ▼

THREATS

overfishing

climate change

bycatch

CONSERVATION EFFORTS ▼

habitat protection

releasing bycatch

BASKING SHARKS

- Basking sharks get their name from their habit of slowly swimming in the sun near the water's surface.

APPEARANCE

Basking sharks are grayish brown to black. Their snouts are long and pointed. Their large gills nearly circle their heads. Their massive jaws contain around 1,500 small, hooked teeth.

SEA MONSTERS?

These sharks often swim together in a line, making them look like one giant animal. Some people who have seen "sea monsters" have likely spotted these sharks swimming together.

SIZE COMPARISON

40FT (12 m)

basking shark

59FT (18 m)

whale shark

4FT (1.2 m)

horn shark

DIET

Basking sharks are filter feeders. They swim slowly with their mouths open, allowing water to flow into their mouths and over their gills. Their gill rakers catch zooplankton and other small invertebrates.

WHERE DO THEY LIVE?

Basking sharks live in cool to temperate oceans and seas around the world. They migrate to follow food.

VULNERABLE SPECIES

▼ VULNERABLE ▼

THREATS

past overfishing practices

climate change

bycatch

pollution

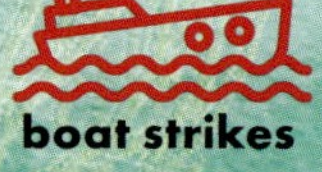
boat strikes

CONSERVATION EFFORTS ▼

creation of protected areas

overfishing laws

managing climate change

WHITE SHARKS

White sharks are top predators. They have one of the strongest bites of all sharks. They are often called great white sharks.

WHERE DO THEY LIVE?

White sharks have one of the largest ranges of all sharks. They live in most temperate and subtropical waters. These sharks migrate seasonally.

DIET

These sharks prefer prey with a lot of blubber to give them energy. They eat seals, sea lions, and porpoises. They often stalk their prey. Then they rush forward to tear prey apart.

SIZE COMPARISON

20FT (6.1 m)
white shark

59FT (18 m)
whale shark

13FT (4 m)
bull shark

APPEARANCE

White sharks are named for their white bellies. Their backs are gray, blue, or brown. They have cone-shaped snouts and jaws lined with seven rows of serrated teeth.

FAMOUS WHITE SHARK

SHREDDER

- **Location:**
Guadalupe Island, Mexico

- **Famous for:**
Shredder was one of the most photographed white sharks. He had a shredded dorsal fin. But he got his name from biting through and completely shredding an anchor line of a diving boat.

WARM-BLOODED SHARKS

Most sharks are cold-blooded. But white sharks are warm-blooded. They can keep their body temperature higher than the water around them.

WHALE SHARKS

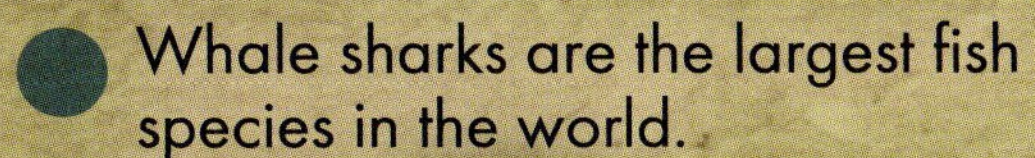

Whale sharks are the largest fish species in the world.

APPEARANCE

Whale sharks have blue, gray, or brownish backs. A pattern of light stripes or spots covers their bodies. Their heads are wide and flat. Barbels hang from each nostril.

BIG MOUTH

Whale sharks have more than 300 rows of tiny, pointed teeth in each jaw. Their mouths are up to 5 feet (1.5 meters) wide!

SIZE COMPARISON

9.8FT (3 m)

broadnose sevengill shark

59FT (18 m)

whale shark

13FT (4 m)

bull shark

WHERE DO THEY LIVE?

Whale sharks live in all warm-temperate and tropical waters except the Mediterranean Sea. They migrate thousands of miles to find food.

DIET

These sharks are filter feeders. They open their mouths wide and suck in water, plankton, and small animals. Food gets caught in their gill rakers as water flows out of their gills.

FAMOUS WHALE SHARKS

STUMPY AND ZORRO

- **Location:** Ningaloo Reef in Western Australia

- **Famous for:** They are the longest-studied wild sharks in the world. Scientists have been tracking them for more than 30 years. They return every year to the Ningaloo Reef to feed.

ZEBRA SHARKS

Zebra sharks get their name from the stripes they have as pups. They are also called leopard sharks because they become spotted as adults.

APPEARANCE

Zebra sharks are dark brown with yellowish stripes and dark spots. Short barbels stick out from their rounded snouts.

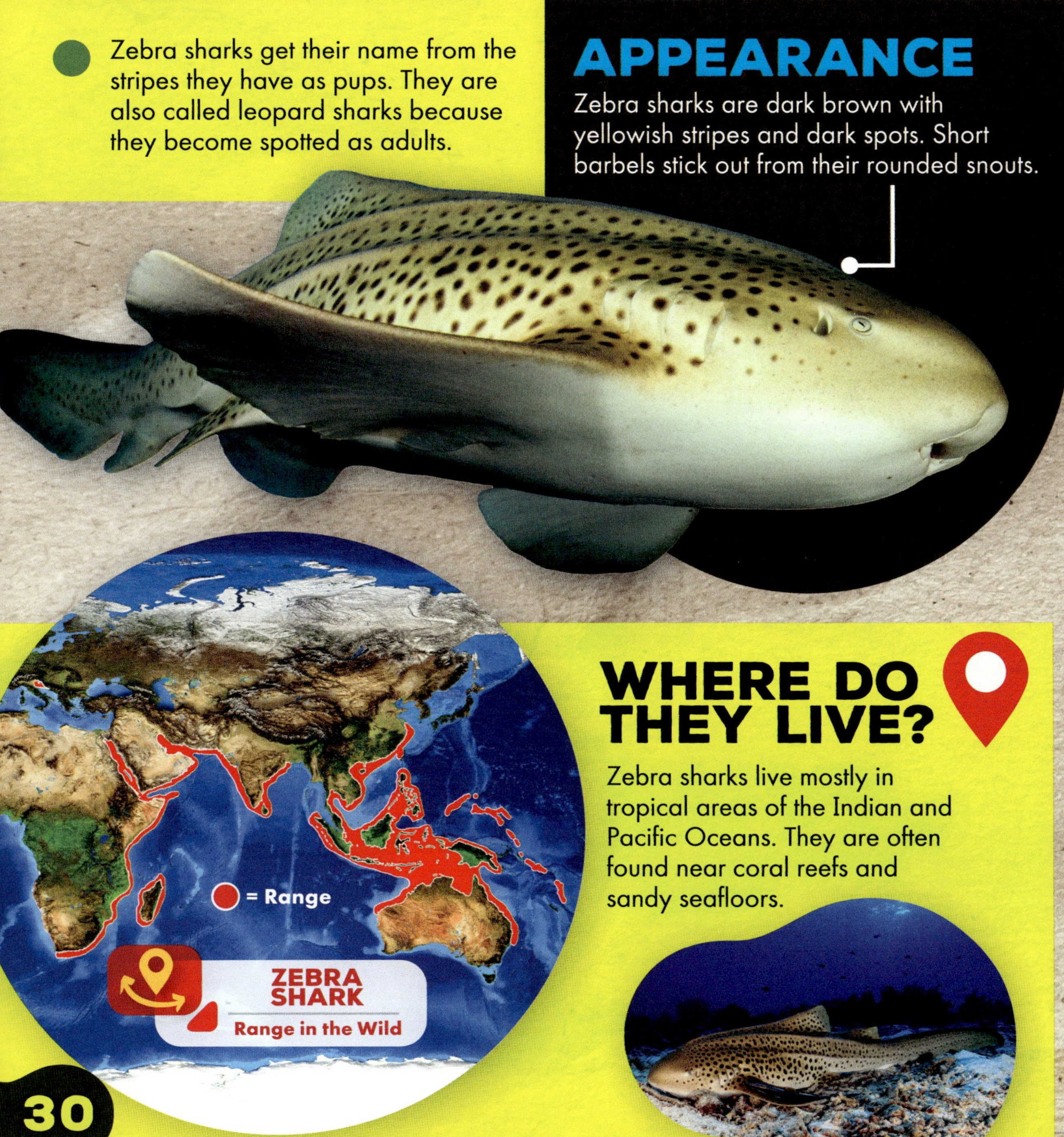

WHERE DO THEY LIVE?

Zebra sharks live mostly in tropical areas of the Indian and Pacific Oceans. They are often found near coral reefs and sandy seafloors.

SIZE COMPARISON

1.6FT (0.5 m)	8FT (2.5 m)	10FT (3 m)

smallmouth cookiecutter shark	zebra shark	Atlantic nurse shark

DIET

Zebra sharks squeeze between rocks and reefs to find hidden small fish and invertebrates. They sense movements with their barbels. Then they suck prey into their mouths.

SHARK OR SNAKE

The tail stripes on zebra shark pups make them look like venomous sea snakes. This helps keep predators away.

VULNERABLE SPECIES

▼ ENDANGERED ▼

THREATS

bycatch

overfishing

shark fin trade

CONSERVATION EFFORTS ▼

repopulation in captivity

tagging sharks to monitor their movement

NURSE SHARKS

Nurse sharks are slow-moving bottom dwellers. There are three species.

DRINK UP

Nurse sharks make a sucking sound as they suck up their prey. They sound like a baby nursing.

DIET

Nurse sharks hunt at night. They gulp up prey using their wide mouths like a vacuum. Common prey include sea urchins, lobsters, and bony fish.

VULNERABLE SPECIES

▼ SHORT-TAIL NURSE SHARKS ▼
CRITICALLY ENDANGERED

SHORT-TAIL NURSE SHARK ▼

THREATS

overfishing

habitat loss

CONSERVATION EFFORTS ▼

programs to increase the population

APPEARANCE

Nurse sharks have flattened bodies and wide heads. They have thin barbels and long tail fins. Their bodies are light or dark yellowish brown.

WHERE DO THEY LIVE?

Nurse sharks swim in warm, shallow waters. Atlantic nurse sharks are found along coasts on both sides of the Atlantic. Tawny nurse sharks live in the Indo-Pacific region, and short-tail nurse sharks live off the coast of eastern Africa.

SIZE COMPARISON

9.8FT (3 m) — broadnose sevengill shark

59FT (18 m) — whale shark

10FT (3 m) — Atlantic nurse shark

SAWSHARKS

Sawsharks have long, sharp snouts that look like saws. Their snouts have special organs called electroreceptors that sense tiny movements made by prey.

BAHAMAS SAWSHARK
Range in the Wild

= Range

WHERE DO THEY LIVE?

These sharks often live in the Atlantic, Indian, and Pacific Oceans.

APPEARANCE

Sawsharks are grayish brown with flattened bodies and heads. Spiracles sit behind their large eyes. Barbels are found halfway down their long snouts.

SPIRACLE

SIZE COMPARISON

13FT (4 m)

bull shark

59FT (18 m)

whale shark

2.8FT (0.8 m)

Bahamas sawshark

BARBELS

DIET

Sawsharks use their specialized snouts to find and defeat prey. They locate small fish and crustaceans with their barbels and electroreceptors. Then they slash their sharp saws side to side to stun and cut prey.

SPECIES PROFILE

BAHAMAS SAWSHARK

- **Range:** Western Atlantic Ocean, near the Bahamas
- **Known for:** These sawsharks live in a limited range. But they live in different habitats, from sandy parts of coral reefs to deeper waters.

SHARK BATTLE

Male sawsharks may fight for a mate. They use their saws to strike one another.

COOKIECUTTER SHARKS

BITE WOUND

Cookiecutter sharks get their name from the round bite wounds they give their prey. There are two species.

SMALLMOUTH COOKIECUTTER SHARK

Range in the Wild

WHERE DO THEY LIVE?

These sharks often live in the Atlantic, Indian, and Pacific Oceans.

TEETHING SHARKS

These sharks swallow their teeth as new ones grow in. This helps increase their calcium levels.

SIZE COMPARISON

40FT (12 m)

basking shark

1.6FT (0.5 m)

smallmouth cookiecutter shark

10FT (3 m)

Atlantic nurse shark

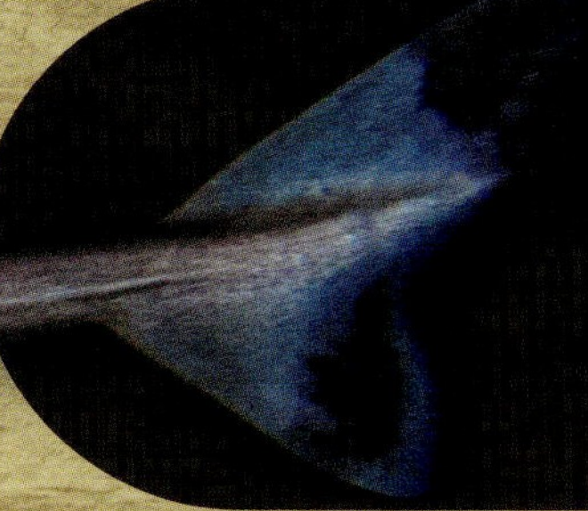

APPEARANCE

These sharks are small and narrow. They are grayish brown with a dark neck band. Their dorsal and pelvic fins often have white-edged tips.

DIET

These sharks attract large animals using bioluminescence. They suction onto prey. Then they spin in a circle as they bite with their wide lower teeth. They also eat small fish, squid, and crustaceans.

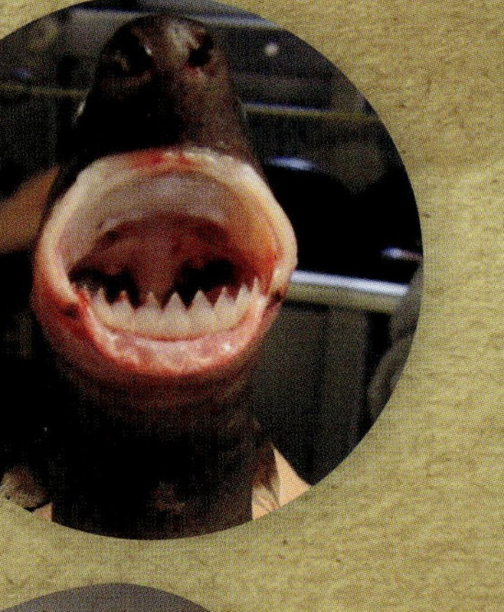

CRUSTACEAN

Bioluminescence in the Ocean

SURVIVAL SKILL

- **What it is:** when a living organism produces and emits light
- **Which sharks use it:** kitefin sharks, pocket sharks, lanternsharks, cookiecutter sharks
- **Why sharks use it:** feeding, mating, and protection

VELVET BELLY LANTERNSHARKS

Velvet belly lanternsharks are small bioluminescent sharks. They get their name from their dark undersides and ability to make light.

APPEARANCE

These small sharks have round bellies, pointed snouts, and long tail fins. They have brown backs and black undersides. Their large eyes reflect green.

DIET

Their glowing bellies help them camouflage from prey. They use their bladelike lower teeth to catch squid, small fish, and crustaceans.

SIZE COMPARISON

1.5FT (0.5 m)

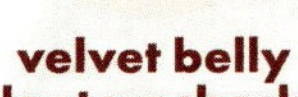

velvet belly lanternshark

20FT (6.1 m)

white shark

13FT (4 m)

bull shark

WHERE DO THEY LIVE?

These sharks are found in the deep waters of the eastern Atlantic Ocean and the Mediterranean Sea.

= Range

VELVET BELLY LANTERNSHARK
Range in the Wild

A LOT OF LANTERNSHARKS

Velvet belly lanternsharks are one of about 50 lanternshark species.

SMOOTH LANTERNSHARK ▲

VULNERABLE SPECIES

▼ VULNERABLE ▼

THREATS

bycatch

climate change

CONSERVATION EFFORTS ▼

no current conservation efforts

COMMON ANGEL SHARKS

Common angel sharks are named for their big, winglike pectoral fins. They are one of more than 20 species of angel sharks.

WHERE DO THEY LIVE?

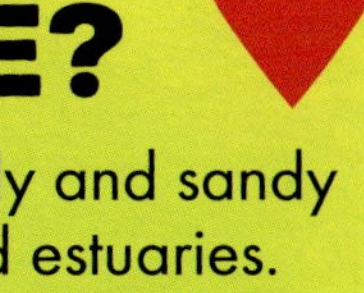

These sharks live in muddy and sandy habitats along coasts and estuaries. They are found in the eastern Atlantic Ocean and the Mediterranean Sea.

DIET

Common angel sharks hide under sand or mud. They wait for prey such as small fish, crustaceans, and mollusks to pass over their heads. Then they attack.

SIZE COMPARISON

8FT (2.4 m)

common angel shark

59FT (18 m)

whale shark

2.8FT (0.8 m)

Bahamas sawshark

APPEARANCE

Common angel sharks have barbels attached to their wide snouts. Their flattened, raylike bodies are tan with dark spots. Two small dorsal fins stick up near their tails.

SUPERFAST

Some angel sharks can grab prey in one-tenth of a second!

▲ JAPANESE ANGEL SHARK

SPECIES PROFILE

ATLANTIC ANGEL SHARK

- **Range:** Atlantic Ocean
- **Known for:** These sharks are blue to gray with white undersides. Their heads and fins have a red tint, with a red spot on their throats and bellies.

SHARKS AND PEOPLE

Sharks have been important to many cultures for thousands of years. In New Zealand and Fiji, sharks are considered godlike and powerful. Hawaiian culture celebrates sharks as protectors of the sea. But other cultures, especially in North America, have long feared sharks. These animals have been shown in books, movies, and television shows as fierce and dangerous.

The terrifying motion picture from the terrifying No. 1 best seller.

JAWS

ROBERT SHAW
RICHARD DREYFUSS
JAWS

FINDING NEMO

THE LITTLE MERMAID

BYCATCH

In the past 50 years, the worldwide shark population has been reduced by over 70 percent. Climate change is altering habitats, changing shark behaviors, and affecting their reproduction. Illegal fishing, overfishing practices, and bycatch are also major threats to sharks.

FOLKLORE PROFILE

NAME:

DAKUWAQA

COUNTRY:

FIJI

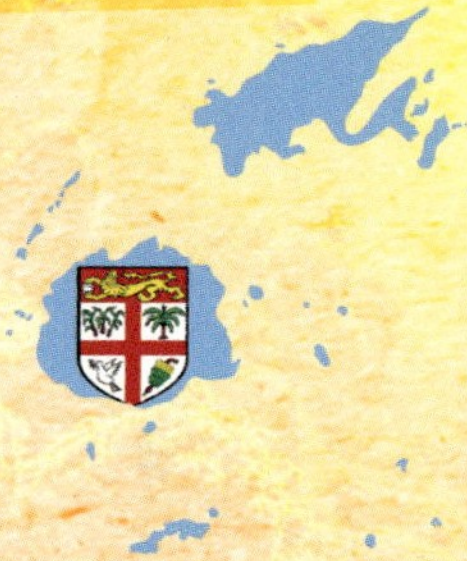

FAMOUS FOR:

Dakuwaqa is an ancient shark god honored in Fiji. Fijian legend says that Dakuwaqa protects humans when they are at sea, especially fishers. He can change form, sometimes appearing to be a human or objects such as logs and stones.

Many organizations are working hard to protect sharks. Some teach people about the dangers of harming shark habitats. Other groups educate people about sharks so that the animals are feared less.

Some organizations work with governments to pass laws that protect these animals and their habitats. These laws include banning illegal fishing, fighting climate change, and outlawing sales of shark fins. Other organizations try to stop overfishing. Taking care of sharks means taking care of ocean ecosystems and keeping nature in balance.

GLOSSARY

adaptations—changes in animals over time that make them better able to hunt and survive

ambush hunters—animals that sit and wait to catch their prey

barbels—whisker-like body parts around the mouths of some sharks that are used to find food

bioluminescence—the ability of a living thing to produce light due to a chemical reaction in the body

bycatch—the unwanted marine animals caught during commercial fishing

cartilage—stretchy tissue that makes up parts of an animal's body

climate change—long-term changes to Earth's weather and climate

cultures—the beliefs, arts, and ways of life in a place or society

denticles—small, toothlike structures that make up a shark's skin

dorsal fin—a fin on top of a shark's back

electroreceptors—tiny holes along the heads of sharks that allow them to sense the movements of prey

estuaries—water passages where tides and river currents meet

evolve—to change from one form into a new form

extinction—the disappearance of a species for good

filter feeders—animals that get food by filtering water currents to obtain tiny plants and animals

gill rakers—comblike structures in gills that trap food

habitats—natural homes of plants and animals

Indo-Pacific—relating to a region that includes both the Indian Ocean and the Pacific Ocean

lagoons—shallow ponds near bigger bodies of water

migrate—to move from one place to another

pectoral fins—a pair of fins on the side of a shark that control a shark's movement

reefs—structures made of coral that usually grow in shallow seawater

scavenge—to feed on carrion; carrion is the rotting meat of a dead animal.

serrated—having a blade like that of a saw

snouts—the noses and mouths of some animals

species—groups of living things that are alike and can reproduce with one another; subspecies are particular types of animals that exist within a species.

temperate—having a moderate climate with no temperature extremes

tropical—related to the tropics where temperatures may be high; subtropical areas border the tropics.

venomous—containing venom, or poison

vertebrates—animals with backbones; invertebrates are animals without backbones.

WRITE ABOUT IT!

- What species of shark would you like to learn more about? **Why?**
- What shark behavior do you think is the most interesting? **Why?**
- **What** are some things you could do to help keep sharks and their habitats safe?

INDEX

The images in this book are reproduced through the courtesy of: frantisek hojdysz, front cover (hammerhead), pp. 3 (top), 16 (bottom), 44 (middle left); David Keep, front cover (whale shark), p. 14 (bottom); Lewis Burnett, front cover (zebra shark), p. 31 (middle right); wildestanimal, front cover (great white), pp. 4 (mako), 9 (great), 15 (threats), 26 (bottom); Timmothy Mcdade, front cover (horn shark); Dudarev Mikhail, front cover (coral), p. 29 (bottom); EwaStudio, p. 3 (bottom); ramoncarretero, pp. 4 (gills), 13 (white); Abstract Aerial Art/ Getty Images, p. 4 (bull); Wonderful Nature, p. 5 (tiger); Pieter De Pauw, p. 5 (white); JJonahJackalope/ Wikipedia, p. 6 (jaw); James St. John/ Wikipedia, p. 6 (tooth); Uryadnikov Sergey, pp. 6 (great), 10 (bottom), 26 (middle), 43 (bottom left); Carlos Grillo, pp. 6 (barbels), 12 (bull), 15 (great), 18 (top); willyam, p. 7; Ollie, pp. 7 (tail), 28 (top); Jonathan, p. 7 (lateral); Jonas Gruhlke, p. 8 (blue); Aquarius Traveller, pp. 8 (pregnant), 11 (whale); Jeff Rotman/ Science Source, p. 8 (newborn); Michael Zeigler/ Getty Images, p. 9 (egg); VisionDive, p. 9 (white); Simon, pp. 9 (basking), 24 (bottom); Richard Carey, pp. 9 (zebra), 30 (top); Sharkdiver Martin, pp. 10 (top), 27; Nature Picture Library/ Alamy Stock Photo, pp. 10 (male), 41 (Japanese), 44 (middle right); scubagreg123, p. 11 (tiger); cbpix, p. 11 (blacktip); Richard, p. 12 (hammerhead); Darin Sakdatorn, p. 12 (tiger); crisod, p. 12 (whale); satou y1, pp. 12 (zebra), 31 (bottom right); Andrea Izzotti, pp. 12 (nurse), 19 (diet), 33 (barbels); Janos, pp. 12 (bullhead), 21 (top left); prochym, pp. 13 (basking), 25 (top, middle), 26 (top), 32 (top); Arzi, pp. 13 (Bahamas), 35 (Bahamas); Blue Planet Archive LLC/ Alamy Stock Photo, pp. 13 (dogfish), 36 (middle); IKER, p. 13 (angel); Steve, p. 14 (scalloped); by wildestanimal/ Getty Images, p. 14 (middle); tephen Frink/ Getty Images, p. 15 (top); Jiri Prochazka, p. 15 (bonnethead); kaschibo, p. 16 (top); Jsegalexplore, p. 16 (appearance); Tropicalens, p. 16 (middle); Wirestock, p. 17 (big); Aaron, p. 17 (bottom); PURNOTA STUDIO, p. 18 (middle); Connect Images/ Alamy Stock Photo, p. 18 (bottom); Michael Patrick O'Neill/ Alamy Stock Photo, p. 19 (left); Martin Prochazkacz, p. 19 (right); Gary Peplow, p. 20 (top); Enessa Varnaeva, p. 20 (middle); Jeremy Francis, p. 20 (bottom); Greg Amptman, p. 21 (top right); HollyHarry, p. 21 (egg case); Kirk Wester, p. 21 (bottom right); Forest2Sea, p. 22 (top); Kelvin Aitken-V& W/ AP Images, p. 22 (bottom); Alessandro De Maddalena, p. 23 (top, bottom right); F1online digitale Bildagentur GmbH/ Alamy Stock Photo, p. 23 (appearance); Tomas Kotouc, p. 23 (bottom left); Stanislav, p. 24 (top); Marko Steffensen/ Alamy Stock Photo, p. 24 (middle); Alex Mustard/ Nature Picture Library, p. 25 (bottom); Lisa, p. 27 (appearance); bilalwebdesigner, p. 28 (appearance); Hoopoe Digital, p. 28 (bottom); Subphoto, p. 29 (middle); Alex, p. 29 (Australia); whitcomberd, p. 30 (bottom); Tatiana Belova, p. 31 (top); SeraphP, p. 31 (middle left); zephyr_p, p. 31 (bottom left); izenkai, p. 32 (middle); Charlotte Bleijenberg, p. 32 (bottom left); Hrr, p. 32 (bottom right); bennymarty, p. 33; Auscape International Pty Ltd/ Alamy Stock Photo, pp. 34 (all), 35 (barbels); shankar s./ Wikipedia, p. 35 (snout); ioworld/ Wikipedia, p. 35 (bottom); YUNOSUKE, p. 36 (bite); PBH/ Alamy Stock Photo, p. 36 (bottom); NOAA Photo Library/ Wikipedia, p. 37 (diet); Aquir, p. 37 (bioluminescence); MWolf Images, p. 37 (crustacean); Andy Murch/ Nature Picture Library, p. 38 (top), 39 (bottom left); Florian Graner/ Minden, p. 38 (middle); Photoshot/ SuperStock, p. 39 (middle); Joacim Näslund/ Wikipedia, p. 39 (bottom right); Peter Verhoog/ Minden Pictures/ SuperStock, p. 40 (top); our wonderful world/ Getty Images, p. 40 (bottom); Sergio Hanquet/ Minden, p. 41 (top); LuisMiguelEstevez, p. 41 (middle left); Smithsonian Environmental Research Center/ Wikipedia, p. 41 (middle right); Roger Kastel/ Wikipedia, p. 42 (Jaws); FlixPix/ Alamy Stock Photo, p. 42 (Finding Nemo); Photo 12/ Alamy Stock Photo, p. 42 (The Little Mermaid); Andreas Altenburger, p. 42 (bycatch); Peter Horree/ Alamy Stock Photo, p. 42 (circle); Rama/ Wikipedia, p. 42 (isolated); Rob Griffith/ AP Images, p. 43 (top, middle); I T S, p. 43 (bottom right); Allen J. Schaben/ Getty Images, p. 44 (top); Emil, p. 44 (bottom left); G. Russel Childress, p. 44 (bottom right).